Beach Hotels

teNeues

Editor:	Martin Nicholas Kunz
Editorial coordination:	Patricia Massó
Introduction:	Christiane Reiter
Translations:	Ade Team, Robert Kaplan (English), Ludovic Allain (French), Margarita Celdràn-Kuhl (Spanish)
Layout & Pre-press:	Thomas Hausberg
Imaging:	Florian Höch, Jan Hausberg

Published by teNeues Publishing Group

teNeues Publishing Company
16 West 22nd Street, New York, NY 10010, USA
Tel.: 001-212-627-9090
Fax: 001-212-627-9511

teNeues Book Division
Kaistraße 18
40221 Düsseldorf, Germany
Tel.: 0049-(0)211-994597-0
Fax: 0049-(0)211-994597-40

teNeues Publishing UK Ltd.
P.O. Box 402
West Byfleet
KT14 7ZF, Great Britain
Tel.: 0044-1932-403509
Fax: 0044-1932-403514

www.teneues.com

ISBN: 3-8238-4566-7

© 2004 teNeues Verlag GmbH + Co. KG, Kempen

Printed in Germany

Bibliographic information published by Die Deutsche
Bibliothek. Die Deutsche Bibliothek lists this publication
in the Deutsche Nationalbibliografie; detailed bibliographic
data is available in the Internet at http://dnb.ddb.de.

Content

Asia | Australia | South Pacific 210

Introduction

Finding a nice beach hotel sounds like the easiest thing in the holiday-world but in fact is one of the most difficult. Because the dream of movie-ripe backgrounds, quietly rustling waves, and an exotic house full of luxury becomes reality only in the most seldom of lucky moments. Whoever has bad luck does not find a paradise by the sea, but has to cross a four-lane highway between the hotel and the water, lean dangerously over the balcony railing to at least sense the promised seaview, or act like a fakir on unsuspected sharp pebbles while sunbathing.

That is not really relaxing. Fortunately, it is also not really unavoidable. One needs to understand that the search for a beach hotel is really just like seeking a synthesis of works of art. The path then leads to unknown shores, to peninsulas, or to tropical bays in which an advertising filmcrew could dance between the hammocks at any moment. At such places, houses await with a view of dense jungles, over softly waving hills, or of an ocean that glows in cobalt blue on sunny days and looks at least like polished silver during the rain. The buildings fit to their surroundings in such a way as if they had always stood exactly here, are built from the stone and wood typical of the country, are furnished with native silk fabrics, or have the exotic fragrance of "their" Spice Island—far apart from the uniform appearance of

many hotels where one doesn't even know if one has woken up in a room in America or Asia. Whoever finds a perfect beach hotel experiences nature, architecture and design in pure harmony.

The expanse of the horizon is reflected in generously designed rooms, the light and air from the beach conjure a very special shimmer onto the interior, charmingly creative details take on the color of a tree trunk, a seashell, or a flower blossom. Ideally, after a few days one no longer even thinks about whether one is inside or outside at the moment, because the indoor and outdoor worlds create a natural unity. Granted—in most cases, such a holiday-universe has its price. But that also allows a dream to become true: The dream of paradise by the sea.

Christiane Reiter

Einleitung

Ein schönes Strandhotel zu finden – das klingt wie die einfachste Aufgabe der Ferienwelt und ist doch eine der schwierigsten. Denn der Traum von der kinotauglichen Palmenkulisse, leise rauschenden Wellen und einem Haus voller Luxus und Exotik wird nur in seltenen Glücksmomenten Wirklichkeit. Wer Pech hat, findet kein Paradies am Meer, sondern muss auf dem Weg zwischen Hotel und Wasser eine vierspurige Schnellstraße überqueren, sich gefährlich weit übers Balkongeländer beugen, um den versprochenen Seeblick zumindest erahnen zu können oder beim Sonnenbad auf ungeahnt spitzen Kieseln Fakir spielen.

Wirklich erholsam ist das nicht – aber wirklich unvermeidbar ist es glücklicherweise auch nicht. Man braucht die Suche nach einem Strandhotel nur als Suche nach einem Gesamtkunstwerk zu verstehen. Dann führt der Weg zu unbekannten Küsten, auf idyllische Halbinseln oder in tropische Buchten, in denen jeden Augenblick ein Werbefilmteam zwischen den Hängematten tanzen könnte. An solchen Orten warten Häuser mit Blick auf dichten Dschungel, über sanft geschwungene Hügel oder auf einen Ozean, der an Sonnentagen kobaltblau leuchtet und im Regen immerhin noch wie poliertes Silber aussieht. Die Gebäude passen sich ihrer Umgebung auf eine Art und Weise an, als hätten sie schon immer genau hier gestanden. Sie sind aus landestypi-

schem Stein und Holz gebaut, mit einheimischen Seidenstoffen ausgestattet oder besitzen den exotischen Duft „ihrer" Gewürzinsel – weit entfernt vom uniformen Erscheinungsbild vieler Hotels, in deren Zimmern man morgens nicht weiß, ob man in Amerika oder Asien aufgewacht ist. Wer ein perfektes gefunden hat, erlebt Natur, Architektur und Design in purer Harmonie.

Die Weite des Horizonts spiegelt sich in großzügig angelegten Räumen wieder, Licht und Luft des Strandes zaubern einen ganz besonderen Schimmer auf die Interieurs, charmant-kreative Details nehmen den Farbton eines Baumstamms, einer Muschel oder einer Blüte auf. Im Idealfall denkt man nach einigen Tagen sogar nicht mehr darüber nach, ob man sich gerade drinnen oder draußen aufhält, denn Innen- und Außenwelt bilden eine selbstverständliche Einheit. Zugegeben, ein solches Urlaubsuniversum hat in den meisten Fällen seinen Preis – aber dafür lässt auch einen Traum wahr werden: den Traum vom Paradies am Meer.

Christiane Reiter

Introduction

Trouver un bel hôtel avec vue directe sur la plage semble l'une des tâches les plus simples du monde des vacances, c'est néanmoins l'une des plus difficiles. Car le rêve du décor sous les palmiers comme on le trouve au cinéma, du murmure des vagues et d'une maison pleine de luxe et d'exotisme ne devient réalité que dans des moments de chance rares. Celui qui n'en a pas ne trouvera pas de paradis au bord de la mer, et sur le chemin entre l'hôtel et l'eau, il lui faudra traverser une route expresse à quatre voies, se pencher dangereusement en avant sur le parapet du balcon pour sentir au moins la vue sur la mer qui lui avait été promise, ou jouer les fakirs sur une plage de graviers incroyablement pointus.

Ce n'est pas vraiment reposant, mais on ne peut heureusement pas non plus l'éviter. Il faut considérer la recherche d'un hôtel sur la plage comme celle d'une oeuvre d'art dans sa totalité. Le chemin nous mène alors à des côtes inconnues, sur des presqu'îles idylliques ou dans des baies tropicales, dans lesquelles pourrait danser à tout moment entre les hamacs une équipe pour le tournage de films publicitaires. Dans de tels lieux attendent des maisons avec vue sur une dense jungle, sur des collines aux courbes douces ou sur un hôtel, qui brille avec la couleur du cobalt les jours de soleil et qui durant la pluie, conserve l'aspect

de l'argent poli. Les bâtiments s'adaptent ici à leur environnement de la sorte qu'on pourrait croire qu'ils ont toujours existé à cet endroit même, ils sont construits en pierre et en bois typiques du pays, équipés d'étoffes de soies indigènes, et imprégnés du parfum exotique de leur île d'épices, loin de l'image uniforme de nombreux hôtels, dans les chambres desquels on ne sait plus si on s'est réveillé le matin en Amérique ou en Asie. Qui a trouvé un hôtel parfait avec vue directe sur la plage vit la nature, l'architecture et le design dans la pureté de l'harmonie.

La profondeur de l'horizon se reflète dans des pièces à l'espace généreux, la lumière et l'air de la plage exercent avec enchantement un éclat bien particulier des espaces intérieurs, des détails à la créativité charmante reprennent les tons de couleurs d'un tronc d'arbre, d'un coquillage ou d'une fleur. Dans le cas idéal, on oublie même au bout de quelques jours que l'on se trouve à l'intérieur ou dehors, puisque les mondes intérieurs et extérieurs constituent une unité évidente. Il nous faut admettre qu'un tel univers de vacances a son prix, dans la plupart des cas, mais qu'il fait aussi devenir un rêve réalité : celui du paradis au bord de la mer.

Christiane Reiter

Introducción

Encontrar un bonito hotel en la playa –suena como algo fácil en el mundo de las vacaciones, pero es una de las cosas más difíciles. El sueño de las palmeras, el susurro de las olas y una casa llena de lujo y exotismo es algo que solamente se hace realidad en casos infrecuentes. Si la suerte no acompaña, junto al mar no se encuentra ningún paraíso, sino que en el camino entre el hotel y el agua tiene que cruzarse una carretera de cuatro carriles, sacar medio cuerpo fuera de la barandilla del balcón para poder ver un poco el mar o tumbarse a tomar el sol sobre un lecho de guijarros puntiagudos como un fakir.

Un panorama nada reconfortante –pero resulta poco menos que inevitable. Buscar un hotel en la playa es una auténtica búsqueda de una obra de arte integral. El camino que lleva a costas inexploradas, penínsulas idílicas o bahías tropicales en las que podría rodarse una película publicitaria entre las hamacas. En esos lugares le están esperando casas con vistas a una densa jungla, sobre colinas de suaves laderas o sobre un mar que en los días de sol reluce de color azul cobalto y en los días de lluvia parece plata pulida. Las construcciones están integradas en su entorno de una forma como si siempre hubiesen estado allí, están construidas con piedra y madera de la zona, decoradas con tejidos sedosos autóctonos o poseen el aroma exótico de "su" isla de

las especias –muy lejos de la uniformidad que muestran muchos hoteles, en cuyas habitaciones por la mañana no se sabe si se está en América o en Asia. Quien haya encontrado un hotel en la playa perfecto, vive la naturaleza, la arquitectura y el diseño en pura armonía.

La amplitud del horizonte se refleja en habitaciones espaciosas, la luz y el aire de la playa embrujan con un brillo muy especial en el interior, los detalles creativos y llenos de encanto toman el tono de color del tronco de un árbol, una concha o una flor. En situaciones idílicas, a veces ya ni siquiera se piensa mucho en si uno está dentro o fuera, ya que el interior y el exterior forman una unidad perfecta. Debe reconocerse que un universo de vacaciones de este tipo tiene su precio en la mayoría de los casos –pero permite convertir un sueño en realidad: el sueño del paraíso junto al mar.

Christiane Reiter

Americas

Hotel Hana-Maui

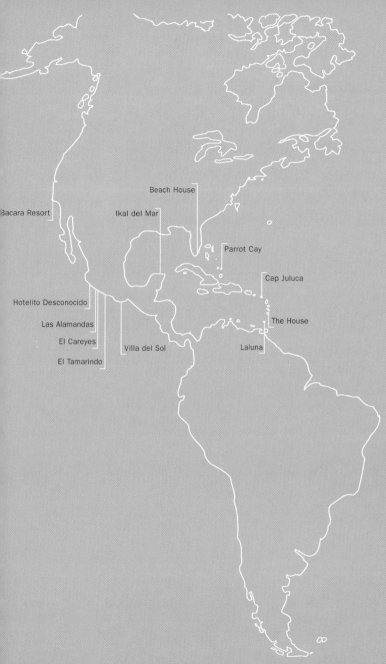

Bacara Resort

Beach House

Ikal del Mar

Parrot Cay

Cap Juluca

Hotelito Desconocido

The House

Las Alamandas

El Careyes

Villa del Sol

Laluna

El Tamarindo

Bacara Resort
Santa Barbara, California I USA

Website	**www.bacararesort.com**
Opening date	**2000**
Address	**8301 Hollister Avenue, Santa Barbara California, 93117 USA**
Phone	**+1 805 968 0100**
Fax	**+1 805 968 1800**
Rooms	**311 rooms, 49 suites, every room features a private patio or balcony, all equipped with high speed internet access and DVD players, half of the rooms with fireplaces**
Description	**located 10 min north of Santa Barbara 2 restaurants, bistro, conference facilities, spa, kid's club**
Architecture/Design	**Hill Glazier Architects, Gary Beggs, Perdian Intl. Landscape Architects**

Bacara Resort   Santa Barbara, California I USA **25**

Beach House

Bal Harbour, Florida I USA

Website	**www.rubellhotels.com**
Opening date	**1999**
Address	**9449 Collins Avenue, Bal Harbour/Surfside Florida, 33154 USA**
Phone	**+1 305 535 8600**
Fax	**+1 305 535 8602**
Rooms	**165 rooms**
Description	**40 min to Miami Airport**
	2 restaurants with ocean terrace, meeting facilities, poolside wellness cabanas, spa
Architecture/Design	**Scott Sanders, Ralph Lauren Group**

Beach House   Bal Harbour, Florida | USA

Hotel Hana-Maui

Maui, Hawaii I USA

Website	**www.hotelhanamaui.com**
Opening date	**1946, reopened 2002, spa 2004**
Address	**5031 Hana Highway, Maui**
	Hawaii, 96713 USA
Phone	**+1 808 248 8211**
Fax	**+1 808 248 7202**
Rooms	**66 rooms including 46 sea ranch cottages, plantation house with full access to all hotel facilities**
Description	**historic resort situated along the eastern shoreline of Maui**
	2 restaurants, lounge, 2 swimming pools, wellness center, yoga, spa
Architecture/Design	**Hunton Conrad**

Parrot Cay

Providenciales, Turks & Caicos Islands | British West Indies

Website	**www.parrot-cay.com**
Opening date	**1999**
Address	**P.O. Box 164, Providenciales**
	Turks and Caicos Islands, British West Indies
Phone	**+1 649 946 7788**
Fax	**+1 649 946 7789**
Rooms	**60 rooms**
Description	**private island, 70 min flight from Miami Airport,**
	speedboat to Providenciales
	private butler service, 2 tennis courts, spa,
	watersports
Architecture/Design	**Keith Hobbs of United Designers**

Cap Juluca

Maundays Bay, Anguilla | British West Indies

Website	**www.capjuluca.com**
Opening date	**1988, full renovated in 2000**
Address	**P.O. Box 240, Maundays Bay**
	Anguilla, British West Indies
Phone	**+264 497 6666**
Fax	**+264 497 6617**
Rooms	**58 rooms and junior suites, 7 suites, 6 pool villas, 18 beachfront villas, some of them with up to 6 rooms**
Description	**20 min by boat and 7 min by air from St. Maarten breakfast served on the private terrace, acqua golf driving range, junior olympic size swimming pool, tennis courts, 2 beaches—2½ miles, water sports, fitnesscenter & spa**
Architecture/Design	**Oscar Farmer, Bob Perkins, Xanadu**

The House

Paynes Bay, St. James I Barbados

Website	**www.eleganthotels.com/thehouse**
Opening date	**2001**
Address	**Paynes Bay, St. James, Barbados**
Phone	**+44 800 587 3427**
Fax	**+44 207 495 5959**
Rooms	**31 suites**
Description	**situated on the west coast of Barbados, 35 min from Grantley Adams International Airport, 20 min from Bridgetown restaurant, bar, open air lounge, library, water sports, butler service available**
Architecture/Design	**Luciano Colombo**

Laluna

Morne Rouge Bay | Grenada

Website	**www.laluna.com**
Opening date	**2001**
Address	**P.O. Box 1500, Morne Rouge Bay, Grenada**
Phone	**+473 439 0001**
Fax	**+473 439 0600**
Rooms	**16 cottages with private plunge pools and large ocean view terrace**
Description	**10 min from international airport restaurant Laluna Kitchen with fine selection of wines, bar, open-air lounge**
Architecture/Design	**Carmelina Santoro, Gabriella Giuntolli**

Hotelito Desconocido

Puerto Vallarta I Mexico

Website	**www.hotelito.com**
Opening date	**1997**
Address	**mail: Carretera a Mismayola 479–205, Edificio Scala, Puerto Vallarta, Mexico, C.P. 48380**
Phone	**+52 322 222 2526**
Fax	**+52 322 223 0293**
Rooms	**28 suites and cabanas, some over the water, rooms without electricity, illumination with candles, solar-powered in-room cooling**
Description	**1,45 hrs south of Puerto Vallarta resort constructed in the style of an old Mexican fishing village, 2 restaurants with traditional Mexican kitchen, spa**
Architecture/Design	**Marcello Murzilli**

Las Alamandas

Puerto Vallarta I Mexico

Website	**www.alamandas.com**
	www.mexicoboutiquehotels.com
Opening date	**1998**
Address	**Las Alamandas Quemaro, Jalisco, Mexico**
Phone	**+52 322 285 5500**
Fax	**+52 322 285 5027**
Rooms	**6 villas with high-pitched tile roofs, private terraces and full-sized living/dining areas**
Description	**2,5 hrs driving from Puerto Vallarta**
	the resort features a private asphalt runway for small aircraft
Architecture/Design	**Isabel Goldsmith, Manuel Mestre**

Las Alamandas   Puerto Vallarta | Mexico **95**

El Careyes
Costalegre | Mexico

Website	**www.mexicoboutiquehotels.com**
Opening date	**1993, refurbished 1999**
Address	**Km 53.5 Carretera Barra de Navidad to Puerto Vallarta, Cihuatlán, Jalisco, 48970 Mexico**
Phone	**+52 315 351 0000**
Fax	**+52 315 351 0100**
Rooms	**56 spacious rooms and suites with terraces overlooking pool or ocean, some with private plunge pools**
Description	**3 hrs south of Costalegre** **restaurant, bar, open air lounge, full-service-spa, tennis courts, water sports**
Architecture/Design	**Diego Villaseñor, Grupo Plan**

El Tamarindo

Costalegre | Mexico

Website	**www.mexicoboutiquehotels.com**
Opening date	**1997**
Address	**km 7,5 Carretera Melaque to Puerto Vallarta Cihuatlán, Jalisco, 48970 Mexico**
Phone	**+52 315 351 5032**
Fax	**+52 315 351 5070**
Rooms	**28 villas, each with private plunge pool**
Description	**ecological reserve, restaurant, bar, lounge, 3 private beaches, 18 hole championship golf course on the property, tennis courts, swimming pool, jungle gym and spa with traditional Temascal (pre-hispanic steam bath)**
Architecture/Design	**Luis Bosoms, Grupo Plan**

El Tamarindo   Costalegre | Mexico

Villa del Sol

Zihuatanejo | Mexico

Website	**www.hotelvilladelsol.net**
	www.mexicoboutiquehotels.com
Opening date	**1978, extension 2002**
Address	**Playa la Ropa S/N, P.O. Box 84, Zihuatanejo**
	Guerrero, 40880 Mexico
Phone	**+52 755 555 5500**
Fax	**+52 755 554 2758**
Rooms	**35 rooms and 35 suites with minipools on their**
	terraces
Description	**150 miles north-west of Acapulco, 12 min from**
	Ixtapa-Zihuatanejo International Airport
	2 restaurants and 3 bars, 4 swimming pools, one
	of them on the beach, 2 x 18 hole golf courses
	10 min away
Architecture/Design	**Helmut W. Leins, Enrique Zozaya**

Villa del Sol   Zihuatanejo I Mexico **127**

Ikal del Mar

Riviera Maya, Mexico

Website	**www.ikaldelmar.com**
Opening date	**2002**
Address	**Playa Xcalacoco, Riviera Maya, Quintana Roo 77710 Mexico**
Phone	**+52 984 877 3000**
Fax	**+52 984 877 3009**
Rooms	**29 villas with private plunge pool, 1 presidential villa**
Description	**30 miles south of Cancun restaurant, bar, swimming pool, full service spa, butler service**
Architecture/Design	**Ramiro Altorre**

Europe

Palm Beach

Tresanton

Kempinski Grand Hotel Heiligendamm

Farol Design Hotel

Maricel

Blu

Hillside Su

Elounda Bay Palace

Almyra

Almyra

Pafos | Cyprus

Website	**www.thanoshotels.com**
Opening date	**2003**
Address	**P.O. Box 60136, 8125 Pafos, Cyprus**
Phone	**+357 26 933 091**
Fax	**+357 26 942 818**
e-mail	**almyra@thanoshotels.com**
Rooms	**190 rooms and suites**
	including Kyma-Suite (page 148)
Description	**the hotel lies directly at the beach, in walking distance to the castle and close to the House of Dionysos with its stunning mosaics**
Architecture/Design	**Joelle Pleot, Tristan Auer**

Kempinski Grand Hotel Heiligendamm

Heiligendamm I Germany

Website	**www.kempinski-heiligendamm.de**
Opening date	**2003, original building 1793**
Address	**18209 Heiligendamm, Germany**
Phone	**+49 38203 7400**
Fax	**+49 38203 7407 474**
Rooms	**107 suites, 118 rooms in 6 buildings**
Description	**2 hrs from Berlin and Hamburg International Airport**
	first German seaside resort, indoor and outdoor restaurants, bar, lounge, meeting facilities, spa and beauty area, 9 hole golf course 5 km away
Architecture/Design	**HPP Düsseldorf, Anna Maria Jagdfeld (Design)**
	original building by Johann Christoph Heinrich von Seydwitz, Carl Severin, Gustav Adolph Demmler

Elounda Bay Palace

Crete | Greece

Website	**www.eloundabay.gr**
Opening date	**built 1976, refurbished 2003**
Address	**Crete, Greece**
Phone	**+302 8410 41502**
Fax	**+302 8410 41783**
Rooms	**230 comfort rooms and bungalows with sea or garden view, 28 family rooms and bungalows with sea view, 5 seafront bungalows, 4 seafront villas, 2 seafront palace suites**
Description	**64 km from Heraklion International Airport, 1,5 km from Elounda Village various restaurants and bars, conference facilities for up to 450 people, amphitheater for up to 600 people, tennis courts, watersport facilities**
Architecture/Design	**Pheodore Giasemakis**

Blu

Mykonos I Greece

Website	**www.ellada.net/grec-mykonos**
Opening date	**1996**
Address	**Mykonos, Greece**
Phone	**+30 2810 300330**
Fax	**+30 2810 300330**
Rooms	**102 rooms including 21 island bungalows, 26 island bungalows deluxe, 34 waterfront bungalows, 5 executive bungalows, many of them with balcony or terrace, some with own pool**
Description	**4 km from Mykonos town restaurant, bar, conference facilities, Aegean decoration**
Architecture/Design	**George Gavalas, Mari Dakalantonakis, Tina Dakalantonakis**

Farol Design Hotel

Cascais | Portugal

Website	**www.cascais.org**
Opening date	**2002**
Address	**Av. Rei Humberto II de Italia 7**
	2750-461 Cascais, Portugal
Phone	**+351 21 482 3490**
Fax	**+351 21 484 1447**
Rooms	**34 guestrooms including suites**
Description	**located in the centre of Cascais, 23 km from**
	Lisbon International Airport
	restaurants, bars, club for 600 people, sun-bed
	terrace, outdoor pool, hammam spa, steam bath
	and roof-top jacuzzi, conference facilities
Architecture/Design	**CM Dias Arquitectos LDA**

176 Farol Design Hotel   Cascais I Portugal

Hotel Maricel

Mallorca I Spain

Website	**www.hospes.es**
Opening date	**2003**
Address	**Carretera de Andratx, No. 11 Cas Catalá**
	07184 Calviá, Palma de Mallorca, Spain
Phone	**+34 971 707744**
Fax	**+34 971 707745**
Rooms	**24 double rooms, 4 suites**
Description	**15 minutes from airport by car**
	restaurant, bar, lounge, terrace with sea view,
	library, pool and wellness area, private landing
	place
Architecture/Design	**Xavier Claramunt**

Hotel Maricel   Mallorca I Spa

Hotel Maricel   Mallorca I Spain **189**

Palm Beach

Gran Canaria I Spain

Website	**www.hotel-palm-beach.com**
Opening date	**2002**
Address	**Avenida del Oasis s/n, 35100 Maspalomas Gran Canaria, Spain**
Phone	**+34 928 721032**
Fax	**+34 928 141808**
Rooms	**327 rooms and suites**
Description	**3 restaurants, one of them gourmet, pool and fitness area in a 1000 year old palm garden, health and wellness centre**
Architecture/Design	**Alberto Pinto**

Hillside Su

Antalya | Turkey

Website	**www.hillside.com.tr**
Opening date	**2003**
Address	**Konyaalti, 07050 Antalya, Turkey**
Phone	**+90 242 249 0700**
Fax	**+90 242 249 0707**
Rooms	**253 rooms, 39 suites, 1 presidential suite, 1 specially designed suite**
Description	**1,5 km from the center of Antalya buffet and á la carte restaurants, beach and sushi restaurants, lounge, bars, ball room, 8 meeting rooms, heated indoor and outdoor pools, spa with treatment and massage rooms, squash, tennis, water sports**
Architecture/Design	**Eren Talu, Yael Bahar, Aslÿ Eke, Merve Yoneyman**

Tresanton

St. Mawes, Cornwall | United Kingdom

Website	**www.tresanton.com**
Opening date	**built 1940, reopened 1999**
Address	**27 Lower Catle Road, TR2 5DR St. Mawes** **Cornwall, United Kingdom**
Phone	**+44 1326 270055**
Fax	**+44 1326 270053**
Rooms	**29 bedrooms including 2 family suites, all rooms** **with views across the sea**
Description	**80 km to Plymouth Airport** **restaurant, bar, lounge, private racing yacht,** **business facilities up to 60 people**
Architecture/Design	**Olga Polizzi**

Asia
Australia
South Pacific

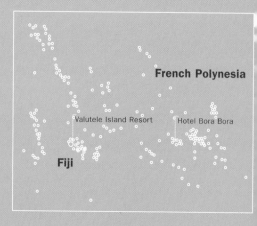

French Polynesia

Valutele Island Resort

Hotel Bora Bora

Fiji

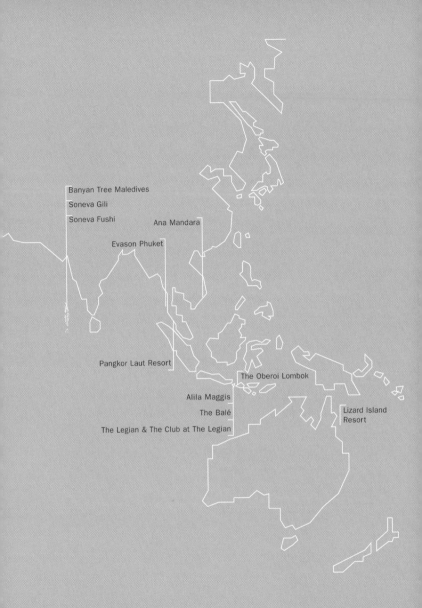

Banyan Tree Maledives
Soneva Gili
Soneva Fushi
Ana Mandara
Evason Phuket
Pangkor Laut Resort
The Oberoi Lombok
Alila Maggis
The Balé
Lizard Island Resort
The Legian & The Club at The Legian

Banyan Tree Maldives

Vabbinfaru, North Malé Atoll | Maldives

Website	**www.banyantree.com/maledives**
Opening date	**1996**
Address	**Vabbinfaru, North Malé Atoll, Maldives**
Phone	**+960 443 147**
Fax	**+960 443 843**
Rooms	**48 villas with a terrace either opening up to the beach or with ocean view**
Description	**beachfront restaurant and bar, garden spa, fully equipped dive center**
Architecture/Design	**Architrave Design & Planning Co., Ltd.**

Soneva Gili

Lankanfushi, North Malé Atoll | Maldives

Website	**www.sixsenses.com**
Opening date	**2002**
Address	**Lankanfushi, North Malé Atoll, Maldives**
Phone	**+960 440 304**
Fax	**+960 440 305**
Rooms	**29 villa suites, 15 residences**
Description	**gourmet restaurant, villa dining, bar, library, pool, tennis courts, health spa, watersport facilities**
Architecture/Design	**Eva Malmstrom Shivdasani**

Soneva Fushi

Kunfunadhoo, Baa Atoll | Maldives

Website	**www.sixsenses.com**
Opening date	**1995**
Address	**Kunfunadhoo Island, Baa Atoll, Maldives**
Phone	**+960 230 304**
Fax	**+960 230 374**
Rooms	**62 villas**
Description	**3 restaurants, beach barbeque, 2 bars, spa facilities with 8 treatment rooms, 3 of them with seaview, diving center**
Architecture/Design	**Dick Wells, Tebott & Wells, Riyan Design Dick, Ismael Rasheed, Eva Malmstrom Shivdasani**

Alila Manggis

Bali | Indonesia

Website	**www.alilahotels.com/manggis**
Opening date	**1997**
Address	**Buitan, Manggis Karangasem**
	80871 Bali, Indonesia
Phone	**+62 363 410 11**
Fax	**+62 363 410 15**
Rooms	**58 guest rooms and suites with ocean view**
Description	**resort nestled in East Bali between the sea and Mount Agung**
	restaurant and cooking school with its own organic garden, bales in rice fields with panoramic view, spa
Architecture/Design	**Kerry Hill Architects**

Alila Manggis Bali | Indonesia **243**

The Balé

Bali I Indonesia

Website	**www.sanctuaryresorts.com**
Opening date	**2002**
Address	**Jalan Raya Nusa Dua Selatan, P.O. Box 76 Nusa Dua, 80363 Bali, Indonesia**
Phone	**+62 361 775 111**
Fax	**+62 361 775 222**
Rooms	**20 Balinese pavilions with pool and private veranda**
Description	**located on a hill overlooking the ocean service by private butlers, foods served al fresco under a gazebo by the main pool, snacks and meals offered round the clock in each pavilion**
Architecture/Design	**Antony Lui, Karl Princic**

The Legian & The Club at The Legian

Bali | Indonesia

Website	**www.ghmhotels.com**
Opening date	**1996, The Club at The Legian 2002**
Address	**Jalan Laksmana, Seminyak Beach, 80361 Bali Indonesia**
Phone	**+62361 730 622**
Fax	**+62361 730 623**
Rooms	**67 suites overlooking the ocean, each with private balcony, 11 villas (10 one-bedroom villas and 1 three-bedroom villa, each with private garden, 10 meter pool and private butler service)**
Description	**situated between rice fields and the beach, restaurant, lobby lounge bar, spa with views of the gardens and beach**
Architecture/Design	**Hadiprana and Associates** **Jaya Ibrahim (Jaya & Associates)**

The Oberoi Lombok

Lombok | Indonesia

Website	**www.oberoihotels.com**
Opening date	**1997**
Address	**The Oberoi, Lombok, Medana Beach, Tanjung P.O. Box 1096, Mataram 83001, N.T.B., Indonesia**
Phone	**+62370 638 444**
Fax	**+62370 632 496**
Rooms	**30 pavilions and 20 villas, many of them with private pool**
Description	**located on the north west coast of Lombok, 45 min drive from Mataram Airport**
	2 restaurants, 40 m swimming pool, dive center, spa with open air massage pavilions
Architecture/Design	**Peter Muller**

Pangkor Laut Resort
Pangkor Laut Island, Lumut | Malaysia

Website	**www.pangkorlaut.com**
Opening date	**1994**
Address	**Pangkor Laut Island, 32200 Lumut, Perak Malaysia**
Phone	**+605 699 1100**
Fax	**+605 699 1200**
Rooms	**148 Malaysian-style luxury villas**
Description	**privately owned island, various restaurants and lounges, 3 tennis courts, 3 pools, gym and spa**
Architecture/Design	**Baldip Singh Bullar, YTL Design Group**

Evason Phuket

Phuket I Thailand

Website	**www.sixsenses.com**
Opening date	**2002**
Address	**100 Vised Road, Moo 2 Tambon Rawai**
	88130 Muang District, Phuket, Thailand
Phone	**+66 76 381 0107**
Fax	**+66 76 381 018**
Rooms	**281 rooms in different categories**
Description	**private beach on Bon Island exclusive to resort**
	guests, 3 pools, 2 volleyball courts, fitness
	center, dive school, health spa, several
	conference rooms
Architecture/Design	**Eva Malmstrom Shivdasani**

Ana Mandara

Nha Trang I Vietnam

Website	**www.sixsenses.com**
Opening date	**1997**
Address	**Beachside Tran Phu Blvd, Nha Trang, Vietnam**
Phone	**+84 58 829 829**
Fax	**+84 58 829 629**
Rooms	**68 villas with veranda**
Description	**restaurant and pool bar, business center for up to 50 people, pool, library, spa, diving center, tennis court and watersports**
Architecture/Design	**Le Long Duc, VIC consultants**

Lizard Island Resort

Lizard Island, Queensland I Australia

Website	**www.lizardisland.com**
Opening date	**2001**
Address	**P.M.B. 40, 4870 Lizard Island, Queensland Australia**
Phone	**+61 292 775050**
Fax	**+61 292 992477**
Rooms	**40 rooms including 18 beach suites and 16 villas**
Description	**27 km off the coast of North Queensland restaurant, bar, lounge, conference rooms, beach club, tennis court, gym and spa**
Architecture/Design	**Desmond Brooks, Susan Rossi**

Vatulele Island Resort

Vatulele Island | Fiji

Website	**www.vatulele.com**
Opening date	**opened 1990, The Point completed 2002**
Address	**Vatulele Island, Fiji**
Phone	**+61 2 9665 8700**
Fax	**+61 2 9665 7833**
Rooms	**18 villas plus premium villa The Point**
Description	**25 min flight from Nadi International Airport dive school**
Architecture/Design	**Doug Nelson, Martin Livingston, Henry Crawford**

Hotel Bora Bora

Bora Bora | French Polynesia

Website	**www.amanresorts.com**
Opening date	**1961, reopened 1989**
Address	**Point Raititi, B.P. 1 Nunue, Bora Bora 98730 French Polynesia**
Phone	**+689 604 460**
Fax	**+689 604 466**
Rooms	**54 Polynesian-style bungalows, 15 overwater bungalows linked to the resort's public areas by walkways**
Description	**located 260 km from the Tahitian capital Papeete, breakfast and dinner are served at the Matira terrace restaurant overlooking the lagoon, 2 bars, lounge, 2 tennis courts, watersport facilities**
Architecture/Design	**Wimberly Allison Tong & Goo**

Africa
Middle East

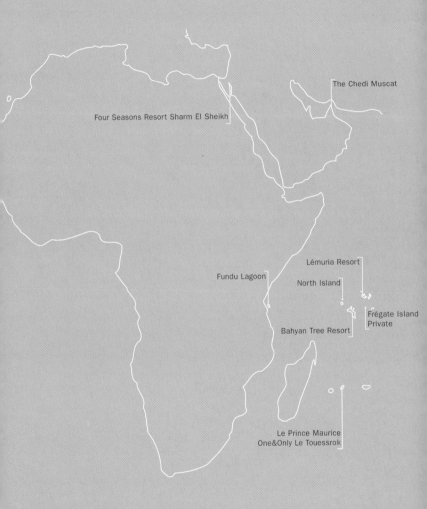

The Chedi Muscat

Four Seasons Resort Sharm El Sheikh

Lémuria Resort

Fundu Lagoon

North Island

Frégate Island
Private

Bahyan Tree Resort

Le Prince Maurice
One&Only Le Touessrok

Four Seasons Resort

Sharm El Sheikh I Egyt

Website	**www.fourseasons.com/sharmelsheikh**
Opening date	**2002**
Address	**1 Four Seasons Boulevard, P.O. Box 203**
	Sharm El Sheikh, Sinai Peninsula, Egypt
Phone	**+20 69 603 555**
Fax	**+20 69 603 550**
Rooms	**136 rooms and suites, some with private plunge pool, 64 family suites**
Description	**located 10 min from Sharm El Sheikh International Airport**
	3 restaurants, grill, 2 lounges, 4 tennis courts, spa and wellness center with lap pool, private spa rooms, outdoor massage areas, coral reef snorkeling and scuba diving, watersport facilities
Architecture/Design	**Hill Glazier Architects, Palo Alto**
	Brayton Hughes Interior Design, San Francisco Architects

Four Seasons Resort   Sharm El Sheikh   Egyt **319**

The Chedi Muscat

Muscat | Oman

Website	**www.ghmhotels.com**
Opening date	**2002**
Address	**North Ghubra 232, Way No. 3215, Street No. 46 Muscat, Sultanate of Oman**
Phone	**+968 50 5035**
Fax	**+968 50 4486**
Rooms	**61 superior and 60 deluxe rooms, 40 suites**
Description	**located at the heart of Oman, 45 min by air from Dubai restaurant, lobby lounge, 2 pools, water-garden, poolside cabanas, private stretch of beach, spa facilities, 2 tennis courts**
Architecture/Design	**Jean-Michel Gathy, Yasuhiro Koichi**

Le Prince Maurice

Poste de Flacq I Mauritius

Website	**www.princemaurice.com**
Opening date	**1998**
Address	**Choisy Road, Poste de Flacq, Mauritius**
Phone	**+230 413 9100**
Fax	**+230 413 9130**
Rooms	**76 junior suites, 12 senior suites, some of them over water, 1 princely suite**
Description	**located on northeast coast of Mauritius, 45 km from the airport**
	2 restaurants, 2 bars, health & beauty center, airconditioned squash court, 2 championship golf courses 10 min away
Architecture/Design	**Jean-Marc Eynaud**

One&Only Le Touessrok

Trou d'Eau Douce I Mauritius

Website	**www.oneandonlyresorts.com**
Opening date	**reopened 2002**
Address	**Trou d'Eau Douce, Mauritius**
Phone	**+230 402 7400**
Fax	**+230 402 7500**
Rooms	**200 rooms and suites**
Description	**located on the east coast**
	3 restaurants, 2 restaurants on neighbouring private islands, bar, Givenchy spa and beauty facilities, new championchip golf course on Ile aux Cerfs endorsed by Bernhard Langer
Architecture/Design	**Macbeth, Ridler Sheperd Low, Hirsch & Bedner Associates**

344 One&Only Le Touessrok   Trou d'Eau Douce | Mauritius

Banyan Tree Seychelles

Mahé | Seychelles

Website	**www.banyantree.com/seychelles**
Opening date	**2001**
Address	**Anse Intendance, Mahé, Seychelles**
Phone	**+248 383 500**
Fax	**+248 383 600**
Rooms	**37 villas including 1 Presidential Villa, each with private pool or outdoor jacuzzi**
Description	**on the southern tip of the island of Mahé, 30 min drive from the international airport 2 restaurants, terrace bar, oriental garden spa**
Architecture/Design	**Architrave Design & Planning Co., Ltd.**

Banyan Tree Seychelles   Mahé | Seychelles **357**

Frégate Island Private

Frégate Island | Seychelles

Website	**www.fregate.com**
Opening date	**1998, health and beauty center 2004**
Address	**Frégate Island Private**
	Seychelles
Phone	**+49 69 8383 7635**
Fax	**+49 69 8383 7636**
Rooms	**16 villas, 14 on top of the cliffs with panoramic views, 2 of them nestled in private gardens for families with children, all with wooden terraces, day bed and jacuzzi**
Description	**private island limited to max. 40 guests to protect the endemic wildlife (turtles, birds), 2 restaurants, bar, private beach, lap pool, gym, newly built health and beauty center**
Architecture/Design	**Wilson & Associates**

Lémuria Resort

Praslin I Seychelles

Website	**www.lemuriaresort.com**
Opening date	**1999**
Address	**Lémuria Resort of Praslin, Anse Kerlan**
	Praslin, Seychelles
Phone	**+248 281 281**
Fax	**+248 281 000**
Rooms	**80 junior suites, 8 senior suites, each positioned**
	15 metres from the shore, nestled in a natural
	botanical garden, all suites with aircondition, tv,
	telephone and VCD/CD systems
Description	**located on the northwest coast of the island,**
	5 min from Praslin airstrip
	3 restaurants, 4 bars, sauna, jacuzzi, children's
	club, 2 tennis courts, golf course
Architecture/Design	**Jean-Marc Eynaud**

North Island

Indian Ocean | Seychelles

Website	**www.north-island.com**
Opening date	**2003, spa 2004**
Address	**North Island, Indian Ocean, Seychelles**
Phone	**+2 48 29 3100**
Fax	**+2 48 29 3150**
Rooms	**11 spacious luxury villas with private lounge, plunge pool, kitchenette, sliding doors allow uniterrupted views, an electro-buggy and two bicycles belong to the equipment**
Description	**"Robinson Crusoe" deluxe private island, 15 min from Mahé by helicopter cuisine with "no menu concept", each menu developed individually by the head chef, sunset beach bar, five beaches including a private honeymoon beach, newly built spa**
Architecture/Design	**Silvio Rech & Lesley Carstens Architecture & Interior Architecture**

Fundu Lagoon

Pemba I Zanzibar

Website	**www.fundulagoon.com**
Opening date	**2000**
Address	**Fundu Lagoon, Pemba, Zanzibar**
Phone	**+255 24 223 2926**
Fax	**+255 24 223 2937**
Rooms	**14 bungalows, rooms equipped with mosquitonets, ensuite bathrooms, one of the bungalows is a beach suite with private chill out deck and plunge pool**
Description	**situated on the south western side of Pemba Island, accessible only by boat restaurant, 2 bars, tv room, massage, fully equipped diving center**
Architecture/Design	**Ellis Flyte**

Photo Credits

Photo Credits	Hotel	Page
courtesy Alila Hotels & Resorts	Alila Manggis	242,243
courtesy Amanresorts	Hotel Bora Bora	306
Amir	Farol Design Hotel	172
courtesy Bacara Resort	Bacara Resort	27
courtesy Banyan Tree Hotels & Resorts	Banyan Tree Maldives	212
Roland Bauer	Alila Manggis Bali	236
	Kempinski Grand Hotel Heiligendamm	150
	The Legian & The Club at The Legian	250
courtesy Blu	Blu	166
courtesy Constance Hotels	Imprint (Lémuria Resort)	3
	Lémuria Resort	374
	Le Prince Maurice	332
courtesy Eleganthotels	The House	60
Francine Fleischer	Parrot Cay	42
courtesy Four Seasons Hotels & Resorts	Four Seasons Resort Sharm El Sheikh	314
courtesy Fundu Lagoon Resort	Fundu Lagoon	392
courtesy GHM Hotels & Resorts	Ana Mandara	286
	The Chedi Muscat	320
courtesy Helios Hotels & Resorts	Elounda Bay Palace	160
courtesy Hospes Hoteles	Hotel Maricel	180
courtesy Hotel Hana-Maui	Hotel Hana-Maui	34
courtesy Hotelito Desconocido	Hotelito Desconocido	80
Martin Nicholas Kunz	Bacara Resort	18
	Banyan Tree Seychelles	350
	Cap Juluca	52
	El Careyes	100
	El Tamarindo	108
	Evason Phuket	276
	Frégate Island Private	362
	Hotelito Desconocido	78
	Ikal del Mar	130
	Laluna	66
	Las Alamandas	90
	North Island	380
	The Legian & The Club at The Legian	256-259
	Villa del Sol	120
courtesy Laluna	Laluna	67,70,73,75
Holger Leue	Hotel Hana-Maui	34
courtesy Mansion Resorts	The Balé	244
C. Michel	Palm Beach	190
Tony Novak-Clifford	Hotel Hana-Maui	34
courtesy Oberoi Hotels & Resorts	The Oberoi Lombok	260
courtesy One & Only Resorts	One&Only Le Touessrok	342
courtesy P&O Resorts	Lizard Island Resort	292
courtesy Pangkor Laut Resort	Pangkor Laut Resort	266
Michael Poliza	North Island	380
courtesy Rubell Hotels	Beach House	28
Robert Radkowski	Hotel Hana-Maui	34
Auggie Salbosa	Hotel Hana-Maui	34
courtesy Six Senses Hotels & Resorts	Soneva Fushi	228
	Soneva Gili	218
courtesy Thanos Hotels	Almyra	142
courtesy Tresanton	Hotel Tresanton	208
courtesy Vatulele Island Resort	Vatulele Island Resort	298
Tamer Yilmaz	Hillside Su	198

Special thanks to:

Maria Jesús Asiain, Bernardo Bertucci, Patrick Brizio, Sheri Broedlow, Wolfgang Burre, Ragini Chopra, Beth Cooper, Trina Dingler-Ebert, Julia Gauci, Fernanda Gembe, Gregor Gerlach, Eustace Guish Guishard, Sophie Hennell, Hans R. Jenni, Thomas Klippstein, Amarin Kocharat, Nina Kumana, Fiona Lane, Lina Lee, Helmut W. Leins, Sylvia Ligonie, Lena Melidoneodi, Thanos Michaelides, Geoffrey Murray, Marcello Murzilli, Laurent A. M. Myter, Olga Polizzi, Victoria L. Pratt, Amanda Pummer, Sonia Redigs, Rui Reis, Christiane Reiter, Abigail Rivera, Diniz Madaleno Rodrigues, Jennifer Rubell, Samir Saab, Emily N. Santos, Anke Schaffelhuber, Frederic F. Simon, Murat Tufan, April Whann, Bea Wolfe, ZFL and www.designhotels.com

Other Designpocket titles by teNeues

African Interior Design 3-8238-4563-2
Asian Interior Design 3-8238-4527-6
Avant-Garde Page Design 3-8238-4554-3
Bathroom Design 3-8238-4523-3
Berlin Apartments 3-8238-5596-4
Cafés & Restaurants 3-8238-5478-X
Car Design 3-8238-4561-6
Cool Hotels 3-8238-5556-5
Cool Hotels America 3-8238-4565-9
Cosmopolitan Hotels 3-8238-4546-2
Country Hotels 3-8238-5574-3
Exhibition Design 3-8238-5548-4
Furniture Design 3-8238-5575-1
Garden Design 3-8238-4524-1
Italian Interior Design 3-8238-5495-X
Kitchen Design 3-8238-4522-5
London Apartments 3-8238-5558-1
Los Angeles Houses 3-8238-5594-8
Miami Houses 3-8238-4545-4
New York Apartments 3-8238-5557-3
Office Design 3-8238-5578-6
Paris Apartments 3-8238-5571-9
Pool Design 3-8238-4531-4
Product Design 3-8238-5597-2
Rome Houses 3-8238-4564-0
San Francisco Houses 3-8238-4526-8
Showrooms 3-8238-5496-8
Ski Hotels 3-8238-4543-8
Spa & Wellness Hotels 3-8238-5595-6
Sport Design 3-8238-4562-4
Staircases 3-8238-5572-7
Sydney Houses 3-8238-4525-X
Tokyo Houses 3-8238-5573-5
Tropical Houses 3-8238-4544-6

Each volume:

12.5 x 18.5 cm
400 pages
c. 400 color illustrations